A New Commandment

Loving As Jesus Loved

by Sharon A. Steele

Aglow Publications
A Ministry of Women's Aglow Fellowship, Int'l.
P.O. Box I
Lynnwood, WA 98046-1558
USA

AGLOW BIBLE STUDIES AND WORKBOOKS

Basic Series

God's Daughter
Practical Aspects of a Christian Woman's Life

Basic Beliefs
A Primer of Christian Doctrine

God's Answer to Overeating
A Study of Scriptural Attitudes

The Call of Jesus
Lessons in Becoming His Disciple

Christ in You
A Study of the Book of Colossians

Triumph Through Temptation
How to Conquer Satan's Lies

Keys to Contentment
A Study of Philippians

Drawing Closer to God
A Study of Ruth

Proving Yourself
A Study of James

Living by Faith
A Study of Romans

The Holy Spirit and His Gifts
A Study of the Scriptural Gifts

Kingdom Living
A Study of New Life in Christ

Coming Alive in the Spirit
The Spirit-Led Life

The Quickening Flame
A Scriptural Study of Revival

A New Commandment
Loving As Jesus Loved

God's Character
A Study of His Attributes

Enrichment Series

Wholeness From God
Patterns and Promises for Health and Healing

Teach Us to Pray
A Study of the Scriptural Principles of Prayer

The Holy Spirit
His Person and Purposes

The Word
God's Manual for Maturity

More Than Conquerors
The Christian's Spiritual Authority

The Beatitudes
Expressing the Character of Jesus

With Christ in Heavenly Realms
A Study of Ephesians

Workbook Series

Introduction to Praise
A New Look at the Old Discipline of Praise

All the Time You Need
The Art of Managing Your Time

How to Study the Bible
Eight Ways to Better Learn God's Word

Spiritual Warfare
Strategy for Winning

Defense Against Depression
The Way to Wholeness

Guidance
Knowing the Will of God

Encourager Series

Restored Value
A Woman's Status in Christ

Invitation to a Party
God's Incredible Hospitality

Write for a free catalog.

Table of Contents

ATTENTION

These studies have been published for the edification of every Christian and may be used by any individual or group. However, unless a Bible study group is part of a local Women's Aglow Fellowship and is under its leadership, the name *Aglow* cannot be used in any way to designate the study group.

Cover design by Ray Braun

Unless otherwise noted, all Scripture quotations in this publication are from the Holy Bible, New International Version. Copyright ©1973, 1978, 1984, International Bible Society. Other versions are abbreviated as follows: KJV (King James Version), TLB (The Living Bible), TAB (The Amplified Bible).

ISBN 0-932305-21-0

Introduction

"A new command I give you: Love one another. As I have loved you, so you must love one another. All men will know you are my disciples if you love one another" *(John 13:34,35).*

Although Jesus has commanded us to love one another, it seems that into every life God allows people who are difficult to love. In addition, we all know people for whom we may have feelings of love, but at times our actions toward them express anger, frustration, and impatience. At other times we may actually feel hatred or disgust for them.

God wants His children to become effective, powerful Christians by learning to love even those who are difficult to love. Often as we attempt to do this, we find ourselves locked into a fierce battle with Satan. Knowing how difficult it is to love those who have hurt us or people we care deeply about, Satan tempts us to be filled with anger, bitterness, and hatred. He knows that as we give in to those natural inclinations, we become ineffective and powerless as children of God.

We can learn to love others with Jesus' kind of love. There will always be times when we don't have any feelings of love toward them, but we must not wait for the right feelings before performing the actions of love. The purpose of this study is to teach us how to love others even when we don't "feel" love for them. It is as we put the practical actions of love into practice that we find the feelings of love following and we become more like Jesus.

Commanded to Love

Introduction

This is the first of three lessons dealing with the tremendous importance of love. As we study God's commandments to love, we will discover the importance of love in God's sight.

Prayer

Dear Father, please open my eyes to see the importance of love. Help me see that to love is Your commandment to me. Help me apply the scriptures in this lesson to my life and give me the willingness to grow more like You. I pray this in Jesus' name and I ask that He will be honored. Amen.

Bible Study

Read **Mark 12:28-34.**

1. What question did the teacher of the law ask Jesus?

   _____

   _____

2. What was Jesus' answer?

   _____

   _____

   _____

   _____

Discussion Question: Why do you think Jesus gave two commands instead of one when the teacher had asked for the one most important commandment?

Both of these commands are of vital importance and are related. If we love God, it greatly increases our ability to love others. If we do not love others, it becomes a barrier between God and us.

3. What did the man say about the importance of love?

_____

_____

_____

_____

4. What was Jesus' reaction to the man's comment?

_____

This man realized that love for God and others is far more important than anything else we can give to God.

Read **Luke 10:25-37.**

5. What question did this expert in the law ask Jesus?

_____

6. How did Jesus answer him?

_____

Discussion Question: Why do you think Jesus answered with a question?

7. In what way did the expert say we are to love God?

_____

8. How are we to love others?

_____

Discussion Questions: What do you think is meant by loving God with all your heart, soul, strength, and mind? What does loving your neighbor as yourself involve?

9. What was Jesus' response to his answer (v. 28)?

Discussion Questions: How does loving God relate to trust in God and salvation? How does loving others relate to your salvation?

Jesus emphasized that loving God is the most important commandment. It is vital to our salvation. Unless we love God, we can't expect to gain eternal life, and unless we first love and accept Him, we can't love others with His kind of love. Loving God enables us to trust Him and to submit to His Lordship. As we love Him and accept His Lordship over us, He enables us to love others.

Personal Questions: How do I love God? How much of myself have I given to Him?

10. What question was asked in verse 29?

11. Why did he ask this question?

Discussion Question: What does his reason tell you about this man?

12. How did Jesus answer his question?

Discussion Questions: Why do you think Jesus used this method to answer his question? What did it accomplish?

13. What actions did the priest and Levite take?

Discussion Question: What do their actions show us about these spiritual leaders?

14. Who stopped to help the man?

15. What practical demonstrations of love did he show?

Discussion Questions: What did it cost him to help? How did he show that he loved his neighbor as himself?

Discussion Questions: Why do you think the priest and the Levite went by without stopping? Give reasons why people today don't help others who are in need. Why do you think the Samaritan helped? What did he gain by helping? How does this story define a neighbor?

In this story the neighbor was not one who lived next door. He was not a friend or even an acquaintance. Instead he was a person who met the need of another. The Samaritan proved his love by giving his time, effort, and money to help meet that man's need. It is sad that often we are too busy or too unconcerned to get involved in the lives of those who need our help. Helping is an action of love. God wants us to be willing to give of ourselves to help those who are in need.

Personal Questions: Am I too busy or too unconcerned to help those in need? How does this story apply to me and the people in my life?

Read **Luke 6:27-31** and **Romans 12:17-21.**
16.   Who does Jesus command us to love in Luke 6:27?

17.   List the three actions of love described in verses 27, 28.

18.   How do the actions in Luke 6:27-31 relate to the instructions in Romans 12:17-21?

19.   What is the main emphasis of these two passages?

Discussion Questions: Why do you think Jesus gave these commands in the Luke passage? What do you think would happen in the life of the person who obeyed these commands? How would his or her feelings be affected? What effect would it have on the other person?

20. What practical action of love is found in Luke 6:31?

_____

_____

Discussion Question: How can this be a test of whether our actions are really actions of love?

Read **Luke 6:32-36.**
21. What actions did Jesus describe that even the sinners do?

_____

_____

22. In what way are Christians to be different?

_____

_____

23. What will be the results of following Jesus' instructions?

_____

_____

24. What do these verses show us about God's kind of love?

_____

_____

Discussion Questions: Why do you think a Christian woman should react differently than the non-Christian toward those who mistreat and abuse her? How do these verses apply to those who hurt the ones we love?

The principles found in these passages from Luke and Romans are among the most powerful in Scripture in teaching us how to love those who are difficult to love. These scriptures are not intended to teach us to become doormats for other people. Instead they teach us the principle of overcoming evil—by doing good. Love is one of God's most powerful weapons against the forces of Satan.

Satan wants us full of anger and bitterness. When others mistreat us or those we love, it is natural to want to retaliate. If we retaliate, the feelings of animosity between us and others grow stronger. However, if we will choose to do good to them, to bless them and pray for them, the feelings of anger and hatred will go away. Often when we pray for those who have hurt us, we ask God to "straighten them up" or to make them act differently. This type of prayer won't cause the same positive results in our lives as one asking God to bless them and meet their needs.

We can't always control our thoughts and feelings, but we can, by an act of the will, choose to respond to those feelings with God's love. If we will choose to pray every time we have a bitter or hateful thought toward another person, those feelings will go away. We need to ask God to show us if there is some action of love that we can perform to help meet that person's need. If we do what He tells us, we will be amazed at the change in feelings. God will be honored and glorified as we show His kind of love.

Personal Application
1. How does this apply to me?
2. Ask God to bring to your attention those who need your help.
3. Ask Him for creative ways to show love and to be helpful.

Memory Work
"But I tell you who hear me: Love your enemies, do good to those who hate you, bless those who curse you, pray for those who mistreat you" (Luke 6:27,28).

Love Shows Our Relationship to God

Introduction

In lesson one we saw that love for God and love for others are God's most important commandments. In this lesson we will see how important loving others is to our relationship with God.

Some of the Scripture passages in this lesson contain very strong wording and could discourage anyone who knows that he/she is failing in loving another. If you are struggling in this area, don't allow these passages to bring despair or cause you to give up. God knows your desire to learn to love, and He will help.

Prayer

Dear God, as I study this lesson, open my eyes to see any bitterness and hatred that might be in my life. Help me to see the seriousness of this problem, and work in me to overcome it. I ask this in Jesus' name. Amen.

Bible Study

Read **Matthew 22:34-40.**

1. What did Jesus say are the two most important commandments?

    _____

    _____

    _____

2. How did Jesus say these two commandments related to the law and the prophets?

    _____

Discussion Question: What do you think verse 40 means?

Read **Romans 13:8-10.**

3.   What debt do we always owe to others?

_____

4.   What does verse 8 say about the person who loves?

_____

Discussion Question: How does obeying the commandment to love fulfill the law?

When we love God with all our heart, soul, and mind, our lives will show honor and reverence to Him. We will want to obey His commands. If we love our neighbors, we will try to help them and bring good into their lives, and we will never seek to harm them in any way.

Read **2 John 5,6.**

5.   How is love for God described?

_____

6.   What is His command to us?

_____

Read **Luke 11:42.**

7.   Although the Pharisees had self-righteously kept many laws, what had they neglected?

_____

Discussion Questions: What do these passages teach about the relationship between love for others and obedience to God's commands? Why is love so important to our relationship with God? If loving is the fulfillment of the law, what is implied when we do not love?

God's commandment to us is to love one another. When we love God, we earnestly seek to love each other. The person who is content to live with hatred needs to recognize that she isn't walking in obedience to God's will.

Read **1 John 2:3-6.**

8.   What is proof that we know God?

_____

9. What is the result of obedience?

10. How should the person who claims to live in Christ act?

Discussion Questions: How does this passage relate to Jesus' commands to love? What role does obedience play in God's love growing in us? Why do you think this is a result? What do you think is meant by verse 5? In what ways should we walk as Jesus walked? How did Jesus' life demonstrate love?

It is important to realize that any area of willful disobedience in our lives is a hindrance to the growth of Jesus' love in us. We cannot grow in the Lord and continue in disobedience. However, we must recognize that love isn't just a feeling. There will be times when we don't have feelings of love and we can't make those feelings happen. At those times we must choose by an act of our will to perform the actions of love. When we do, God will take away feelings of hatred, and we will be acting in obedience to His commands. Obeying Jesus' command to love involves performing the actions of love even when the feelings aren't present.

Read **1 John 1:5-7.**
11. What does it show when a professing Christian walks in darkness?

Read **1 John 2:9-11.**
12. What do these verses tell us about the person who hates?

13. What do they tell us about the person who loves?

14. What is promised to the person who lives a life of love?

Discussion Questions: What do you think is meant by ''the darkness'' and "the light"? Verse 10 is a key to victorious living. Why do you think love is important if we are to live a victorious life in Christ? What does verse 10 imply about hatred in our life?

Darkness refers to any area that is in Satan's control. The light refers to any area controlled by God. We need to recognize that if we have an area of hatred in our lives, Satan has control of us in that area. This hatred will become a stumbling block, and we won't be able to live victoriously until we get rid of it.

Personal Questions: Has hatred in your life ever caused you to stumble and fall in your Christian walk? Can you share this with your group? Has love for another helped you to be victorious?

Read **1 John 3:10-20.**
15. What two characteristics are an indication that a person is not a child of God (v. 10)?

_____

_____

16. What is the message we have heard from the beginning (v. 11)?

_____

17. What does love for others show us according to verse 14?

_____

18. What is the spiritual condition of one who doesn't love?

_____

19. What is the connection between hatred and murder?

_____

Discussion Questions: Why do you think such strong emphasis is placed on the effects of hatred? What do these verses show us about hatred and our relationship to God?

Hatred is a devastating force, consuming a person. When a Christian allows hatred to dwell in her life, it severely hinders her capacity to experience God's love. These scriptures may seem harsh, but we need to recognize the terrible danger we face if we allow hatred to grow in our lives.

20.   What example of love are we given (v. 16)?

_____

21.   What action of love is encouraged (v. 17)?

_____

22.   What does it show when we don't act in love toward the brother in need?

_____

23.   How are we encouraged to love (v. 18)?

_____

24.   What are the results of loving others?

_____

_____

Discussion Questions: How do you think verse 16 applies to Christians today? What actions of love could be acts of obedience to verse 16? How could this affect the use of our time, energy and material possessions?

These verses show that love is not just feelings or words. Love expresses itself in action. When we express our love with actions, the beautiful results are assurance that we belong to God and a marvelous peace in God's presence.

Read **1 John 4:7-21.**
25.   Who is the source of love?

_____

26.   List all the phrases in this passage that pertain to the person who loves.

_____

_____

_____

27. What do they tell about our relationship to God (v. 21)?

_____

28. List the phrases that pertain to the person who doesn't love.

_____

29. What do they tell about his relationship with God (v. 20)?

_____

_____

30. List all the phrases that show the results of love.

_____

_____

_____

_____

31. How did God show His love for us (v. 9)?

_____

_____

32. What should our response to God's love be (v. 11)?

_____

Discussion Question: Why do you think it is impossible to love God and hate our brother?

We need to recognize that a person doesn't become a child of God by loving others. A person becomes a child of God by accepting Jesus as Lord and Savior. Love for others is an indication that the person is a true believer and that God's love is active in her life.

When we love God and put Him first in our lives, He removes the hatred from our hearts and replaces it with His love. When someone hurts us or those we love, feelings of hatred may come, but we must realize that hatred is a consuming emotion and that hatred toward another person greatly reduces our capacity to love. We have the choice of either feeding our feelings or choosing to get rid of them. If we feed those hateful feelings, they will overcome us, and our relationship to God and to others will be adversely affected. We will be unable to experience a close relationship with God. However, if we choose to react to the hurts by returning actions of love, God will remove those feelings of hatred and fill us with His love and peace.

Personal Application

What do your actions show about your relationship to God?

1. Are you experiencing hatred that is hindering your fellowship with God?
2. Do you choose to get rid of those feelings and replace them with actions of love?
3. Ask God to show you specific actions of love that you can perform toward those you are having difficulty loving.
4. Write down any actions that He reveals to you and then write down the date that you perform these actions.

Memory Work

"Whoever loves his brother lives in the light, and there is nothing in him to make him stumble" (1 John 2:10).

Lesson Three

The Power of Love

Introduction

In this study, as we look at scriptural promises to those who love, we will discover the great power of love. We will also see the promised results in the lives of those we love and discover some of the sad results of Christian service without love.

Prayer

Lord, as I study this lesson, help me to grasp the promises that You make to those who love. Make me aware that these promises are for me. Examine my life and bring to my attention any areas where I am not showing Christ's love to others. Make my life a demonstration of Your love. I ask this in the name of Jesus Christ our Lord. Amen.

Bible Study

Read **Colossians 2:2,3.**
1. What was Paul's twofold intention for these people (v. 2a)?

_____

_____

2. With what results?

_____

_____

Read **Colossians 3:14.**
3. What result of love is found in this verse?

_____

Discussion Question: What role do you think love plays in uniting people and why?

Love is God's most powerful force to draw people together into unity. Love that enables us to accept others even with their faults is essential to perfect unity.

Read **Ephesians 4:11-14.**
4. List all words or phrases which describe the mature Christian.

_____

_____

_____

_____

5. Now list words or phrases describing the immature Christian.

_____

_____

Read **Ephesians 4:15,16.**
6. How are we to speak?

_____

7. With what results?

_____

_____

8. How is the church (the body) built up?

_____

9. What phrases indicate that each individual has a responsibility in church growth?

_____

Discussion Questions: How do you think love affects the spiritual growth of a body of believers? How does love affect the growth in numbers? What happens to a body of believers when love isn't present or expressed?

Read **Luke 11:17.**
10. What tragic result of division is found here?

_____

Discussion Question: How does this apply to a home? A fellowship?

Love has the power to unite, and it is only through love that a body can be built up. A united, loving body is one of the signs of a Spirit-filled church or a Spirit-filled home. *"The fruit of the Spirit is love..." (Gal. 5:22).* When a body of believers is growing in Christ, it is also growing in unity and love. A fighting, bickering, unloving body shows that God's spirit is not in control.

It is important to realize that a home or a church will build itself up in love as each member does its part. Each of us should realize that we have a vital part in the growth of Christ's Body. Each job is important; each person is important. It is vital that each person do her part to help the Body grow.

Personal Questions: What is my responsibility to the body of believers? What can I do to help Christ's Body grow? How can I express love to those in my church or in my home? What can I do to help bring a spirit of unity?

Read **John 13:34,35.**
11. What result of love is found here?

_____

Discussion Questions: Why do you think that this result occurs? What do you think is the result to the world when Christians don't show love for each other?

The world doesn't have the capacity to love the unlovely or to love those who hurt them. When we are able to reach out in love to those difficult people, the world will recognize that we are different. This difference will show them that we belong to Jesus.

Read **John 17:20-23.**
12. What phrase indicates that you are included in Jesus' prayer?

_____

_____

13. What is Jesus requesting from the Father?

_____

14. List all the phrases that suggest Christians are to be united and loving each other.

_____

_____

15. What results are shown for the world?

_____

_____

Discussion Question: Why do you think love for each other would have such an impact on unbelievers?

Love is God's greatest magnet to draw the world to Himself. People everywhere desperately want and need to be loved. When the world sees Jesus' kind of love and acceptance among believers, people will want to belong. Our love for each other is proof to the world that Jesus came and that He loves them. Too often we try to shame or condemn people into a right relationship with God, but we must love them into His kingdom. Love, as expressed in the Gospel, is God's power to draw people to Himself.

Personal Questions: Do you know of an unbeliever or a defeated Christian that you can, through love, help bring into a right relationship with Him? Ask God for creative ways to show and express love toward that person.

Read **1 John 3:18-20; 1 John 4:17,18.**
16. List all phrases from these two passages that suggest results of loving one another.

_____

_____

_____

_____

Discussion Questions: What do you think is meant by 1 John 3:17? (See James 2:14-17.) How do words fit into our expression of love? Why do you think actions of love will set our hearts in God's presence? Why do you think love drives out fear?

It is important to realize that words of love are not being condemned in these verses. Often people need to hear our expressions of love. There are times, however, when words simply aren't enough. When a person has a physical, spiritual, or emotional need that we can aid in meeting, true love will express itself by helping to answer those needs.

When we perform actions of love, one result is a sense of assurance that we belong to God. Sometimes our hearts condemn us and make us feel guilty even when God hasn't condemned us. Satan is the accuser of Christians (Rev. 12:10), and he delights in a guilt-ridden, defeated child of God. One way in which the Christian receives peace and assurance of salvation is through actions of love toward others.

Read **1 John 3:21-24.**
17.   How do these promises relate to verses 18-20?

_____

_____

_____

18.   What conditions are given for receiving these promises (v. 22)?

_____

_____

19.   What commands must we obey according to verse 23?

_____

_____

Discussion Questions: How does love affect our prayer life? How do obedience and faith affect our prayer life?

Love is a condition to having prayers answered. We must believe in Jesus, and we must love one another. If we have love in our hearts for others, we are much more likely to feel confidence in approaching God. If we're experiencing hatred, it is extremely difficult to draw into God's presence. Faith and obedience are also important. Without faith, we limit God's power in our lives. (See Matthew 13:58.) If we are deliberately disobedient, we're ashamed to draw into His presence, and our prayer life is severely hindered.

Personal Questions: How do these verses apply to your prayer life? What are you promised? Are there changes in your life that you need to make before you can have power in prayer? Are you willing to make those changes?

Read **John 15:9-14.**

20. How has Jesus loved us?

_____

21. What are we told to do?

_____

22. How is this accomplished?

_____

23. What results are promised to us?

_____

_____

24. What is Jesus' command?

_____

25. What example of love is given?

_____

Discussion Questions: How does love for others affect your joy? What happens to your joy when you are experiencing hatred toward another? How does obedience to Jesus' commands affect your joy?

Loving others is essential to experiencing God's joy. There is nothing that can rob us of joy in the Lord faster than hatred. It is impossible to harbor unresolved anger, hatred, or bitterness and still experience the joy of the Lord. They cannot co-exist.

Personal Questions: Are ill feelings toward another or any disobedience toward God robbing you of the joy and peace that Jesus came to give. Will you confess these to God and ask for His strength to gain victory?

Read **1 Corinthians 13:1-3.**

26. List the gifts and manifestations of the Holy Spirit from these verses.

_____

_____

27. What is the result when a person has these spiritual gifts but lacks love?

_____

_____

_____

Discussion Questions: Why do you think these gifts are so ineffective if not accompanied by love? Why do you think so many people seek spiritual gifts rather than trying to build love into their lives?

Often as Christians we deeply desire spiritual gifts. Although spiritual gifts are desirable, we need to realize that unless they are accompanied by love, their value to us and to Christ's Body will be greatly diminished. We must learn to love or these gifts will accomplish little. To be powerful and effective to the kingdom of God, the gifts of the Spirit must be combined with the active love of Jesus in our lives.

Personal Questions: Is my desire to increase the love in my life, or am I mostly seeking spiritual gifts? What are my spiritual gifts accomplishing for Christ's kingdom?

28. List the results of love promised in this lesson.

_____

_____

_____

_____

_____

_____

Personal Application
1. Which results do you desire to see increased in your life?
2. Will you ask God to show you ways to build and demonstrate more love in your everyday life?

Memory Work
"Let love and faithfulness never leave you; bind them around your neck, write them on the tablet of your heart. Then you will win favor and a good name in the sight of God and man" (Prov. 3:3,4).

The Source of Love

Introduction

It's easy to see that God has commanded us to love and that our love for others is an indication of our relationship with God. It's also easy to see that love has tremendous power. However, sometimes it's extremely difficult to love another person, and our lack of love can cause terrible feelings of guilt and failure. The remaining lessons will give definite actions we can take to build and demonstrate love into our lives.

Prayer

Lord, fill me with Your Holy Spirit so that Your love can overflow to everyone in my life. Teach me how to live daily by the power of Your Spirit. I ask this in the name of Jesus. Amen.

Bible Study

Read **1 John 4:7,8,16.**
1. What is the source of love?

2. How is God described in verses 8 and 16?

3. What does verse 7 tell us about the person who has been born of God?

Discussion Question: What do you think is meant by being born of God?

It is important to realize that God is both love and the source of love. It is only as we believe in Jesus that we are born of God's Spirit, and His love becomes active within us. As we accept Him, His Spirit indwells us and begins to renew us. It is His Spirit within us that enables us to love others and gives us a desire to reach out to them.

Read **Galatians 5:13-26.**

4. What instructions are given in verse 13?

_____

_____

5. What does verse 14 teach about love?

_____

6. What actions are we warned against in verse 15?

_____

7. What results from those actions?

_____

Discussion Question: What do you think ''biting and devouring'' means?

8. What is the key to overcoming these actions?

_____

9. What does the sinful nature desire?

_____

10. Summarize the struggle between the sinful nature and the spiritual nature.

_____

11. What is the solution?

_____

Discussion Questions: How does the promise in verse 16 relate to that struggle? What do you think is meant by the phrase, ''live by the Spirit''?

12. List the acts of the sinful nature.

_____

_____

_____

_____

_____

Personal Questions: Will you ask God to reveal to you any of those actions that may be present in your life? Will you confess them as sin and ask God to cleanse you?

It is important to recognize that the sin nature is always present in our lives and that it is in conflict with the spiritual nature. It is a natural tendency of the flesh to respond to hurtful situations with hatred, discord, and fits of rage. Apart from the power of God's Spirit, we cannot respond with love. In our own strength, we can't overcome these natural tendencies toward sin. It is only when we live by the power of God's Spirit that we are able to overcome them.

13. List the fruit of the Spirit.

_____

_____

Personal Questions: Which of the fruit of the Spirit are most evident in your life? Which are least evident?

Discussion Questions: How do you think we can cultivate the fruit of the Spirit in our lives and help them grow?

Read **John 15:1-18.**
14. List all phrases that show the futility of trying to bear spiritual fruit through human strength and effort.

_____

_____

_____

15. What is promised to the one who remains or abides in Jesus?

_____

_____

_____

_____

16. What is the tragic result of not remaining or abiding in Jesus (v. 6)?

_____

_____

Discussion Questions: What do you think is meant by remaining or abiding in Jesus? What is the individual's responsibility? How does this passage relate to the fruit of the Spirit?

It is essential that we recognize that God is the source of love and that love is a fruit of God's Holy Spirit. It is only as we remain in Jesus that we are able to bear the fruit of God's Spirit. When His Spirit fills and controls our lives, the natural result is love toward others and a growth of the fruit of the Spirit.

Although God is the One who produces the fruit of the Spirit, there is also an element of human responsibility. We cannot expect to grow in the Spirit unless we are feeding the spiritual nature with frequent worship, prayer and Bible study. Neither can we expect growth if we are in willful disobedience to God. Remaining or abiding in Jesus implies a day-to-day and minute-by-minute relationship with Him. Without that close relationship, we cannot produce the fruit of the Spirit.

Many people experience a very dramatic filling of the Holy Spirit. Following that experience they see much evidence of the fruit of the Spirit in their lives. Tragically, many expect that one experience to carry them on a spiritual high indefinitely. They don't feed the spiritual nature and they make no effort to grow in the Spirit. The result is spiritual disaster. They are weak and ineffective; they have no joy in the Lord and no victory and live as defeated Christians. Unfortunately, too often, they bring dishonor to the name of Jesus and to the reputation of the Holy Spirit. God wants us to keep on being filled with His Spirit.

Read **Romans 5:5.**
17. What result of the Spirit-filled life is found here?

_____

_____

Read **2 Corinthians 3:17,18.**

18. How does this relate to our ability to love?

_____

_____

_____

19. After each of the following verses, summarize what it says about living a victorious, fruitful life in the Spirit.

Matt. 26:41 _____

_____

1 Pet. 2:2 (KJV) _____

_____

John 15:10 _____

_____

Eph. 3:16-21 _____

_____

_____

_____

_____

_____

_____

_____

Personal Questions: Which of the above verses indicates an area of needed growth in your spiritual life? Which promise is most meaningful to you? Is a condition given as a requirement for fulfilling that promise? If so, what is it? Do you need to make any changes to be able to claim that promise?

The power of God is available to us through His Holy Spirit. We have the power to live a fruitful, effective life, filled with God's love. However, if we try to do it in our own strength, we will fail. We must lay hold of

God's power by being continuously filled with His Spirit. It is only by the power of God's Spirit that we can produce the fruit of the Spirit.

We cannot expect a one-time experience to empower us for life. In the book of Acts we see that the disciples of Jesus were filled with the Spirit over and over. Ephesians 5:18 commands us to be filled with the Spirit. The Greek word that is used for *filled* is in the continuous present tense. The literal translation is "Be you being filled." The verb tense implies that we are to be filled with God's Spirit NOW and we are to be continuously being filled. We need to seek God daily and to ask for His continuous filling and empowering. It is only as we draw near to God and let His Spirit continually fill and control us that we are able to love those who are difficult to love. If it is your desire to grow in your ability to love, strengthen your relationship to God. Keep on being filled with the Spirit.

Personal Application
1. Is there an area of willful disobedience that is hindering the work of God's Spirit in your life?
2. Will you ask God to reveal to you any such disobedience?
3. Will you confess that sin and turn away from it?
4. Will you seek the continuous filling of God's Holy Spirit?
5. Will you ask Him to fill you and in faith believe that He will?
6. Are you willing to make time spent with God a priority in your life? What steps will you take to do this?

Memory Work
"God has poured out his love into our hearts by the Holy Spirit, whom He has given us" (Rom. 5:5b).

Love Is Accepting

Introduction

This study is the first of three lessons dealing with Jesus' kind of love. In it, we will see how Jesus' love accepts us even with our faults and weaknesses. It is as we receive Jesus' love and acceptance toward us that we are able to reach out in love and acceptance to others.

Prayer

Dear Lord, help me to receive the love and acceptance that You have given me. Teach me how to love those who have values different than mine. Show me how I can treat them with respect and acceptance. Reveal to me any areas of unrealistic expectations that are preventing me from accepting others. I ask this in the name of Jesus Christ our Lord. Amen.

Bible Study

Read **John 13:34,35.**
1. How did Jesus command His disciples to love?

   _____

2. What would be the result of that kind of love?

   _____

   _____

Discussion Question: How would you describe Jesus' love toward us?

Read **Romans 5:8.**
3. How is the love of God demonstrated?

   _____

4. What phrase implies that Jesus' love is accepting?

    _____

5. What do the following verses tell about God's love and acceptance?

    John 3:16,17_____

    _____

    _____

    _____

    1 John 3:1 _____

    Eph. 2:4-9_____

    _____

    _____

    _____

Read **Luke 15:11-31.**
6. Briefly summarize this story.

    _____

    _____

    _____

    _____

Discussion Question: What actions of the younger son would make it difficult to accept him?

7. How did the father demonstrate his love and acceptance of his son even before the son asked forgiveness?

    _____

8. How did the father show that he accepted him as a son?

    _____

_____

_____

Discussion Questions: How do you think the son felt as he drew close to home? How do you think he felt as he saw his father running toward him? Why do you think the father was able to treat the son this way?

9.   How did the older brother react to his brother's return?

_____

_____

Discussion Questions: How did the older brother's actions show his lack of love toward his brother? What do you think would have happened to the younger brother if the father had acted the way the older brother did? What does the parable show about the love of God?

The love of God is beautifully portrayed in this parable. The younger son had made a real mess of his life and had undoubtedly caused his father much grief and sorrow. Yet his father was not looking at his own hurts. The son was still a long ways off, but he had turned his heart toward his father. The father saw him coming, and, in great love, he *ran* to meet him where he was.

In the same way God's love for us is an accepting love. He doesn't wait for us to be perfect before He loves us. When God sees a repentant heart, He comes to meet us right where we are. He accepts us as *His* children because of His love, mercy and grace. It is very difficult for any person to reach out in love to another unless that person first feels the acceptance of God. God loves us and His love accepts us. He longs to draw us into His arms of love just as the father in this story loved his wayward son.

Personal Questions: Do you feel that you have made a mess of your life? Do you realize that God's love accepts you even with your shortcomings? Will you thank God that He saw beyond your faults and accepted you as His child? Is there someone you know who has made a real mess of his or her life? Do your actions toward them resemble the actions of the father in the parable, or are they the actions of the older son?

Read **Romans 14:1-12.**
10.   What are we commanded to do (v. 1)?

_____

_____

11.   Why are we commanded not to look down on others?

_____

12.   What do verses 9-12 teach us about judging?

_____

_____

13.   What is the usual reason why people judge others (vv. 5,6)?

_____

14.   What is the important consideration concerning the special days we observe and the foods we eat?

_____

These people had a difference of opinion. Some had come from a strong Jewish background and held certain days as sacred occasions. These days had no special significance to the Gentile believers. There was also a question of whether the meat found in the markets had come from animals that had been used in sacrifice to pagan gods. As a result, some refrained from eating meat altogether. Others believed that since pagan gods had no power, there was no harm in eating the meat and enjoying it. They thanked God for it. Both of these groups felt the actions they had chosen were correct.

Paul emphasizes that because both groups had chosen their actions in honor to God, God had accepted the actions of both. A problem arose when one group did not accept the other. They judged each other, not because they were wrong, but because they were different.

Discussion Questions: What issues today might be similar to the questions of special days and unclean foods as seen in this passage? What attitudes do we need to demonstrate toward the person whose actions are different than ours?

Read **Romans 14:13-23.**
15.   What instructions are given in verse 13?

_____

_____

_____

16. How does verse 15 relate to the instructions in verse 13b?

_____

_____

_____

Reread **verses 15, 20, and 21.**
17. What important action of love is described in these verses?

_____

_____

Discussion Questions: How can our actions destroy the work of God? What is the proper relationship between freedom in Christ and love for each other?

Read **Romans 15:1-7.**
18. What actions of love are described in verses 1 and 2?

_____

_____

_____

19. What key to unity is found in verse 5?

_____

_____

20. What does verse 7 command and what will be the result?

_____

_____

Discussion Questions: Why is following Jesus important if we are to come to unity with each other (v. 5)? How does the Scripture help us during difficult times in our relationships with others (v. 4)? What does it mean to accept one another as Christ has accepted us? Why do you think accepting one another will bring praise to Jesus?

Accepting weaknesses in others is not common to human nature. Human nature wants people to change to fit our standards before we will accept them. When we are able to accept others with their faults, it will bring honor and praise unto Jesus. It is only as we follow Jesus and gain the encouragement and hope of the scriptures that we will be able to accept others in spite of their weaknesses.

Read **Ephesians 5:33.**

21. What are husbands and wives instructed to do?

_____

_____

_____

Discussion Question: How do you feel that acceptance relates to respect for a person?

Read **Luke 6:37-45.**

22. List the phrases in verses 37, 38, that show a specific action and a result that follows that action.

Action	Result
_____	_____
_____	_____
_____	_____
_____	_____
	_____
	_____
	_____

23. What do verses 41 and 42 teach us about condemning?

_____

_____

_____

_____

Discussion Questions: What characteristics do you find hardest to accept in others? Are these traits present in your own life? What do you think is meant by the statement, "For with the measure you use, it will be measured to you"? How does that statement relate to love and acceptance? To judgment and condemnation?

All of us want to be loved and accepted by others. It is important to realize that it is only as we love and accept others that they are able to love and accept us in return. If we are critical, condemning people, people will be critical and condemning of us. If we are loving and accepting, we will be loved and accepted.

Personal Questions: Am I treating others with acceptance? Am I judging and condemning? Am I forgiving?

24.   What important truth concerning our words and actions is found in verse 45?

_____

_____

_____

Frequently, we want to respect people. We want to accept them, but it is impossible unless we are thinking of them with respect and acceptance. We often come into certain relationships with unrealistic expectations. As a result, we tend to make mental lists of their shortcomings and failures. We repeatedly go over these lists in our minds and they grow longer and longer. Then because we want to be loving, we try to speak or act with respect and acceptance. It doesn't work. We fool no one. A person knows when you accept and respect him and can tell if you are insincere.

The only way we can sincerely treat a person with respect and acceptance is to change our way of thinking about that person. We need to ask God to show us how He sees that person and to show us that person's good qualities. Then we can make a list of every good quality that God brings to our remembrance and daily thank God for these good qualities. We can also show our appreciation to the person for the qualities that are commendable.

As we focus on the good qualities, we will find that sincere feelings of respect and acceptance are growing within us. Our actions toward that person will begin to demonstrate sincere respect and acceptance. As our actions and attitudes change, the other person will sense that and will be free to grow and develop more good qualities.

Sometimes our expectations of ourselves are even more severe than our expectations of others. We often do not like ourselves because we can't live up to our own unrealistic expectations. We need to ask God to show us our good qualities and begin to focus on those. Then God will build us up, and our good qualities will grow.

Read **Philippians 4:8.**

25. What should be the focus of our minds?

_____

_____

_____

Personal Application

1. Will you ask God to show you how He sees a person that you are having difficulty accepting?
2. Will you ask Him to show you that person's good qualities?
3. Will you make a list of these qualities and daily thank God for the good in this person?

Memory Work

"Accept one another, then, just as Christ accepted you, in order to bring praise to God" (Rom. 15:7).

Love Is Forgiving

Introduction

Jesus has commanded us to love one another as He has loved us. In this lesson we will see that Jesus' love toward us is a forgiving love, and we will see the beautiful results of forgiveness, as well as the tragic results of unforgiveness.

Prayer

Dear Father, thank You for the forgiveness that is mine in Christ Jesus. Open my eyes to see any areas of unforgiveness in my life. I pray in the name of Jesus that You will help me deal with any unresolved anger and show me how to get rid of it. If there is someone I need to forgive or someone I need to ask forgiveness from, reveal him to me as I study Your word. I ask for a willingness to act upon what You show me. Amen.

Bible Study

Read **1 Corinthians 13:4-7.**
1. What phrase implies that love is forgiving?

_____

2. What do the following passages teach us about Jesus and forgiveness?

Matt. 9:1-8_____

_____

_____

Luke 7:36-50_____

_____

_____

John 8:2-11 _____

_____

Jesus loved others with a forgiving love. He lovingly forgave those whom the world had classed as terrible sinners. It is important to realize that no sinner is so bad that Jesus' love cannot forgive.

3. What do the following passages teach about Jesus' forgiveness?

    Eph. 1:3-7 _____

    _____

    1 John 1:8-10 _____

    _____

Just as Jesus forgave sin when He lived upon the earth, He still forgives all who will put their trust in Him. No matter how terrible our sin may be we have the promise of 1 John 1:9: If we confess our sin, He will forgive and He will cleanse. Christians do not have to be weighed down with guilt. We can claim the forgiveness of Jesus Christ and realize that through the acceptance of Jesus, we are holy and blameless in God's sight (Eph. 1:4).

Personal Question: Have you asked Jesus to forgive you? If you have an unconfessed sin standing between you and God, confess it right now. Then claim the forgiveness that is yours in Christ Jesus. Thank God that He sees you as holy and blameless because of Jesus' sacrifice of love.

Read **Matthew 26:67,68; 27:26-31.**
4. List the ways that Jesus was mistreated.

    _____

    _____

    _____

Read **Luke 23:32-34.**
5. How did Jesus react to the mistreatment He received?

    _____

    _____

    _____

Discussion Questions: Why do you think Jesus was able to respond the way He did? What effect do you think His forgiving attitude had on those who had mistreated Him?

In some way we don't understand, forgiving seems to release the power of God to work in another's life. It's interesting to note that less than two months after Jesus had asked God to forgive those who had mistreated Him, 3,000 people were saved in one day. Possibly many of those 3,000 were the same people who had been in Jerusalem screaming for Jesus' crucifixion. They had mocked Him, they had spit on Him, they had even crucified Him. But He had asked God to forgive them. Love is forgiving. Jesus was able to respond to cruel mistreatment with the forgiveness that comes from love. His love, which manifested itself in forgiveness, had a life-changing effect on those for whom He prayed.

It is often difficult to forgive those who have hurt us. It is sometimes even more difficult to forgive those who have hurt the people we love. One way that we can build a forgiving spirit is to choose by an act of the will to pray for that person who has caused the pain. Jesus prayed for those who were hurting Him. If we will choose to pray for the person who has hurt us or those we love, we will find that forgiveness begins to grow within us. The anger and the hurts begin to heal as we pray for the offender.

Read **Colossians 3:12-14.**
6. List the instructions regarding forgiveness.

_____

_____

_____

7. What needs to be added to bring perfect unity?

_____

Discussion Question: What do you think it means to "forgive as the Lord forgave you"?

Personal Question: If there is someone you need to forgive, will you ask God to reveal it to you?

Read **Ephesians 4:25-32.**
8. What instructions does Paul give regarding anger?

_____

_____

9. What is the result of the improper handling of anger (v. 27)?

_____

10. How are we to speak?

_____

_____

11. What are we urged to not do in verse 30?

_____

12. What are we urged to eliminate?

_____

_____

13. How are we to treat each other?

_____

14. What phrase indicates how we are to forgive?

_____

Discussion Questions: In what ways do you think anger can give Satan a foothold in our lives? How does verse 29 apply to anger? How do the actions in verse 31 relate to the instructions in verse 26: "In your anger do not sin"? When do you think anger is sin? When is it not sin? How do you feel our handling of anger could grieve the Holy Spirit?

We need to realize that anger is a natural human emotion. Although it is not necessarily sin, if we allow it to hurt others, it becomes sin. Likewise, if we don't get rid of anger, it will often turn into bitterness and hatred. Anger is often a hindrance to feelings of love, and we must learn to deal with it.

Communication is often a key to working through conflict and anger. When we attack another, the doors to communication are usually closed. When expressing our anger, we need to apply the principle of "speaking the truth in love" (Eph. 4:15). We must never allow words spoken in anger to destroy another. It is important to learn to express our hurts and our feelings without attacking. We also need to be sensitive to the hurts that the other person is experiencing. We need to listen to each other.

When communicating our anger, we need to pray first and then in an attitude of humility and kindness go to the other person involved. We need to realize that we may have also caused hurts to that person, and we may need to ask their forgiveness for the pain we have caused. If we only attack, telling others how badly we've been hurt, we may get rid of our anger, but we leave others bitter and angry instead. God's plan is that we be united in a love that forgives, rather than divided by anger.

Read **2 Corinthians 2:5-11.**
15. List the reasons why Paul urged the Corinthians to forgive.

_____

_____

16. What would their forgiveness demonstrate (v. 8)?

_____

Discussion Questions: Why do you think unforgiveness would result in the offending party being overwhelmed by excessive sorrow? If someone has offended the church, how do you think unforgiveness would affect him? How do you think unforgiveness allows Satan to outwit us?

An unforgiving attitude toward a person can cause that person to be overwhelmed by sorrow to the point of giving up. Unforgiveness will hurt the other person, but we need to realize that it also leaves the door open for Satan to outwit us. An unforgiving heart is dangerous. It can damage both the person who is unforgiven and the one who refused to forgive.

Read **Matthew 6:12-15.**
17. Tell why these verses teach about forgiving others and about forgiveness from God.

_____

_____

_____

_____

It is important to realize that a bitter, unforgiving spirit shows a serious break in our relationship with God. Those who will not forgive others cannot experience the forgiveness of God. As a result, the unforgiving person will often have tremendous feelings of guilt. As long as we carry unforgiveness, we continue to experience the hurts. When we forgive, the healing of those hurts can begin.

Read **Hebrews 12:15.**
18. What result of unforgiveness is found here?

_____

_____

Discussion Questions: How can bitterness cause trouble and defile many?
How does bitterness show that we have missed the grace of God?

Read **Luke 6:27-37.**
19. List phrases that imply actions of forgiving love toward those who
      have hurt us.

_____

_____

_____

_____

_____

_____

Personal Application
1. Reread Luke 6:27-37 and ask God to show you a specific act of forgiv-
    ing love He wants you to perform toward someone who has hurt you
    or one you love.
2. If you have an angry, unforgiving spirit toward anyone, will you ask
    God for the desire and the strength to forgive?
3. Will you choose by an act of the will to forgive?
4. Will you begin to pray for that person you need to forgive?

Memory Work
_"Bear with each other and forgive whatever grievances you may have against
one another. Forgive as the Lord forgave you. And over all these virtues
put on love, which binds them all together in perfect unity"_ (Col. 3:13,14).

Love Is Sacrificing and Serving

Introduction

Jesus' love for us is a sacrificing, serving love. He left the splendors of heaven to suffer and die, to meet our greatest need. This kind of love is never self-centered nor arrogant. Jesus' love is giving and serving, and we are commanded to love others as He has loved us.

Prayer

Dear Father, help me to see Your sacrificing love for me. Open my heart to accept Your great love that I might be able to give that same kind of love to others. Help me see areas of selfishness that are hindering the growth of love in my life. Amen.

Bible Study

Read John 15:12-15.
1. What did Jesus command us to do?

2. What is the greatest expression of love?

Discussion Question: How did Jesus love us?

Read 1 John 4:10-12.
3. How is love defined?

4. What should we do because of God's great love for us?

_____

5. What does it show when we love each other?

_____

_____

Discussion Questions: How is Jesus' sacrifice a demonstration of genuine love? Why does accepting God's love make it easier to love one another?

The greatest expression of love is the giving of one's self for another. Jesus showed His love toward us by giving His life to bring us salvation. His love, which demonstrated itself in His great sacrifice, has made eternal life available to each of us.

Read **Ephesians 5:1,2.**
6. What instructions are we given in verse 1?

_____

7. What kind of life are we to live?

_____

8. How are we instructed to love?

_____

Discussion Question: How does loving with a sacrificial love relate to being an imitator of God?

Read **John 13:1-5, 12-17.**
9. What did Jesus know according to verse 1?

_____

10. What did He show His disciples?

_____

11. What was Jesus' position and authority?

_____

12. What action of love did Jesus perform?

Discussion Questions: What do you think that Jesus' washing of the disciples' feet showed? How does His greatness relate to His willingness to become a servant?

13. What had the disciples called Jesus?

14. What was His response to those titles (v. 13)?

15. What instructions did Jesus give?

16. What promise is found in verse 17?

17. What is the condition for receiving that promise?

Discussion Questions: How do you think this passage applies to Christians today? What are some practical ways that we can serve each other? How do you feel when you do something to help another? What truth do you think Jesus was trying to emphasize in verse 16?

The task of washing the feet was traditionally done by the lowliest of servants, yet Jesus, the Lord and Master, showed His great love to His disciples by taking the position of a servant. In washing their feet, He gave to all believers a beautiful example of love in action. Love is willingly being a servant. Love does not seek to exalt self, but to serve others. Love does not ask, "How much must I do?" Love asks, "How much can I do?"

Often people try to exalt themselves, feeling that if others would recognize their position and their worth, they could be happy. Verse 17 emphasizes that it is as we serve others that we are blessed. When we serve others, our own sense of self-worth grows. It is in humbling ourselves and serving others that we are exalted. If you are struggling to love another person, ask God to show you ways that you can serve that person. As you willingly seek to serve and to meet that person's needs, your feelings of love will grow with each action.

Read **Philippians 2:1-11.**

18.   What attitudes and actions are encouraged in this passage?

_____

_____

_____

_____

_____

19.   What attitudes and actions are discouraged?

_____

_____

20.   How is Jesus described in verse 6?

_____

21.   List the phrases that show what Jesus became for us.

_____

_____

_____

_____

22.   What phrases show that Jesus had a choice?

_____

Discussion Questions: In what ways do you think our attitude should be like that of Jesus? How does this passage relate to the renewing of the mind? (See Romans 12:1,2.) What practical steps can you take to renew your mind and develop the attitude of Jesus? How does the attitude of Jesus relate to sacrificing and serving?

Jesus left the glories of heaven and humbled Himself even to the point of dying a criminal's death. He gave up all splendor and honor to meet our greatest need. His actions left us the ultimate example of sacrificing and serving love.

We cannot respond with Jesus' kind of love unless we develop the same attitude that Jesus had. This can be developed only by spending time in His presence and in His word, allowing Him to renew our minds.

Often when struggling in relationships, the problem is that our minds are focused on *our* unmet needs. Focusing on those needs tends to make them seem larger, and we become increasingly unhappy. As we seek to develop the mind of Christ, we need to change our focus from our unmet needs to meeting the needs of others. This doesn't necessarily mean that we will attempt to satisfy their every desire because that might not be what they really need. However, if we will try to meet their *needs*, we will find that our needs are also being met, or God will graciously change our needs to bring us peace and joy where we are. If we make meeting our needs our priority, those needs will never be met. When we try to meet the needs of others, we find joy, contentment, and a feeling of love growing within us.

Personal Application
1. Is there someone you are having difficulty loving?
2. Are you willing to show that person love by putting his/her needs above your desires?
3. Are you willing to show that person love by becoming a servant?
4. Will you ask God to show you specific actions of service that He wants you to perform?

Memory Work
"Be imitators of God, therefore, as dearly loved children and live a life of love, just as Christ loved us and gave Himself up for us a fragrant offering and sacrifice to God" (Eph. 5:2).

Lesson Eight

Love Is Kind and Builds Up

Introduction

In this lesson we will see that love treats others with kindness. One of the most needed acts of love is that of building each other up. Many people who are difficult to love have poor self-images and they cannot reach out to love others unless someone first reaches out to them with a love that builds up.

Prayer

Lord, please make me aware of the unkind actions in my life. Teach me how to replace unkind words and deeds with actions that are kind and build others up. I pray this in the name of Jesus Christ our Lord. Amen.

Bible Study

Read **Jeremiah 31:3,4a.**
1. How is God's love described in this passage?

_____

Read **1 Corinthians 13:4-7.**
2. What phrases from these verses describe kindness as an action of love?

_____

Read **2 Peter 1:3-9.**
3. What has God given us (vv. 3,4)?

_____

_____

_____

4. What key to power is found in verse 3?

Discussion Questions: How do verses 3, 4 promise the strength to live a life of love? What role does God's Spirit play in living that life of victory? What do you think the phrase *"through our knowledge of him"* (v. 3) means? How can we grow in our knowledge of Him?

To those who know Jesus as Lord and Savior, God promises everything we need to live a life of godliness. He promises the power to participate in His divine nature and escape the world's corruption. In giving us these assurances, God promises us the power to love. To grow in our knowledge of the Lord, we need to spend time with Him in worship, prayer, and Bible study. Obedience is also a key to knowing Jesus better. (See John 14:21.)

5. What phrase from verse 5 indicates the individual responsibility in Christian growth?

6. What character qualities need to be added to faith?

7. What phrase implies a growing Christian (v. 8)?

8. What is the result of these qualities growing in our lives?

Discussion Questions: How can we add these qualities to our lives and help them to grow? How does unkindness keep a Christian from being effective and productive? How can kindness increase our effectiveness?

It is important to realize that even though God has given us everything we need for godliness, we have a responsibility to put out every effort to grow in godly attributes. It is as we draw into God's presence and submit ourselves to Him that we increase in our knowledge of Him and become more like Him.

Read **2 Timothy 2:22-24.**
9. What do these verses say we should pursue?

10. What kinds of arguments are we to avoid and why?

_____

_____

11. What qualities should the Lord's servant possess?

_____

_____

Discussion Questions: Do you feel that all arguments are foolish and stupid? Why or why not? What is the difference between an argument and a quarrel? How can quarreling lead to unkindness and resentfulness? How can quarreling make one's teaching ineffective? Who are the people in your life that you are teaching? Why is kindness so important if you are going to be an effective teacher?

Kindness is one of the most important factors in our being effective as teachers in our homes and in our churches. Children learn so much from the attitudes and actions of their parents. A child who is treated with kindness learns to be kind. A person who is trying to teach about God will be totally ineffective unless that teaching is combined with the actions of kindness. A lack of kindness in the teacher often leads to rejection of the teaching.

Read **1 Peter 3:1-12.**
12. List the actions of kindness found in these verses.

_____

_____

_____

_____

13. What is required of a person who wants to love life and see good days?

_____

_____

_____

14. What phrase indicates that living peaceably is not always easy?

Discussion Questions: How do you think our words influence the pursuit of peace in our lives? How would controlling the tongue contribute to a person's loving life and seeing good days?

Read **Titus 2:3-5.**
15.　What was Titus encouraged to teach the older women?

16.　What were the older women to teach the younger women?

17.　What would be the result of the women learning these things?

Discussion Questions: What do you think is meant by the phrase "so that no one will malign the word of God"? How does unkindness bring disrespect to God? How does kindness bring Him glory?

Kindness is a fruit of the Spirit and an action of love. One of the ways we most often express kindness is by our words. Unfortunately, our words are also often used to express cruelty and unkindness. God wants us to pursue love and to pursue peace. One of the most effective ways to do this is to speak words of kindness.

Read **1 Corinthians 8:1.**
18.　What does love do?

Discussion Question: How do you think the action of love described here relates to our words?

Read **1 Thessalonians 5:8-11.**

19.   What qualities are we encouraged to have?

_____

20.   What phrases indicate these qualities are a protection?

_____

21.   What actions should be a result of God's love toward us?

_____

Discussion Questions: How do you think faith, love, and the hope of salvation can protect us from Satan's attacks? How can we increase those qualities? Discuss practical ways to apply the instructions in verse 11.

Read **Ephesians 4:29-32.**

22.   What kind of talk should not come out of our mouths?

_____

23.   What guidelines for beneficial speech are found in verse 29?

_____

_____

_____

24.   What actions of love are described in verse 32?

_____

Discussion Questions: How do the instructions in verses 31, 32 relate to the commands in verse 29? What do you think it means to grieve the Holy Spirit? When do our words grieve the Holy Spirit?

25.   What do the following verses teach us about our words?

   2 Tim. 2:16 _____

_____

_____

Prov. 18:21 _____

_____

Prov. 16:24 _____

_____

Prov. 15:4 _____

_____

_____

Prov. 15:1 _____

_____

Prov. 12:18 _____

_____

Love is kind and love builds up. Our words can be kind or cruel. They can build up or tear down. Often those people who are the most difficult to love are those who have low self-esteem. They are incapable of reaching out in love to others because they do not love themselves. One of the most needed actions of love toward those people is the need to build them up. If you know such a person, ask God to show you her actions that are worth respect and for which you can honestly be grateful. Tell her how much you appreciate each good quality within her. Expressing appreciation in this way will help you to focus upon the best in that other person, and it will be of tremendous help in building that person up.

Discussion Questions: What are some practical ways that you can encourage and build up your husband? Your children? Your friends? Your fellow workers? Others in your church or fellowship? What can you do to help encourage yourself?

As you make the building up of another person your goal, that person will often begin to feel better about herself. This causes her to be able to accept herself and she usually will become easier to love. When you are seeking to build another person up, God will also give you increased feelings of love toward that person. Let us make love that is kind and builds up a part of our way of life.

Personal Application
1. Will you ask God to show you someone who needs your encouragement?
2. Will you ask Him to reveal to you practical ways that you can build that person up?
3. Write down what He reveals to you.
4. Will you act upon what He shows you?

Memory Work
"Do not let any unwholesome talk come out of your mouths, but only what is helpful for building others up according to their needs, that it may benefit those who listen...Be kind and compassionate to one another, forgiving each other, just as in Christ God forgave you" (Eph. 4:29,32).

Love Covers Over and Is Patient

Introduction

Hatred sees every fault, and magnifies and complains about it, but love covers over a multitude of sins, is patient and does not give up during difficult times. God has made some beautiful promises to those who persevere.

Prayer

Blessed Father, thank You that the precious blood of Jesus has covered over my sin. Enable me to love others with a love that covers over their sin. Help me to not give up when it is difficult to love. Thank You for Your promises to me. I pray this in the name of Jesus. Amen.

Bible Study

Read **1 Peter 4:8.**
  1. What phrase shows the importance of love?

  _____

  2. What action of love is described in this verse?

  _____

Discussion Questions: What do you think is meant by the phrase "love covers a multitude of sins"? How and why do you think this happens?

Read **Hebrews 9:11-26.**
  3. What does verse 12 indicate that Jesus did for us?

  _____

  _____

  _____

  _____

4. List the results of Christ's sacrifice (vv. 14,15)?

_____

_____

_____

5. What phrase in verse 22 indicates why the Israelites used blood in their worship to cover over everything?

_____

_____

6. What was the result of Christ's sacrifice (v. 26)?

_____

Discussion Question: How is Jesus' sacrifice a demonstration of the kind of love that covers over sin?

The love of God sent Jesus to earth to give His life as a sacrifice for our sin. Although sin separates us from God (Isa. 59:2), the perfect sacrifice of Jesus provides a way for us to be brought back into fellowship with God. Hebrews 9:22 emphasizes that without the shedding of blood there can be no forgiveness of sin. Jesus shed His blood to provide forgiveness. His love, which led Him to be sacrificed for us, covers over our sin.

Read **2 Corinthians 5:14-21.**
7. For whom did Christ die?

_____

8. What else has Christ done for us (vv. 18,19)?

_____

_____

_____

9. What did Christ become for us and what is the result?

_____

_____

58

Discussion Questions: How are these verses a demonstration of love that covers over sin? What do you think is meant by the phrase *"we might become the righteousness of God" (v. 21)?*

Read **Isaiah 61:10.**
10.   What phrases indicate God's love covers over sin?

_____

_____

_____

   When Jesus died on the cross, He paid the penalty for our sin, by becoming sin for us, and in exchange He gave us His robe of righteousness. When God looks at the believer, He looks at her through the blood of Jesus, and He sees her as righteous. God's love covers over our sin. When we accept Christ's love and forgiveness toward us, it helps us to accept ourselves. As we see Jesus' love accepting us and covering over our sin, we are more able to reach out in love toward others.

Personal Questions: Have you accepted the love of Christ that covers sin in your life? Do you realize that as a believer you are seen by God as righteous because of your faith in Jesus?

11.   What do the following verses from Proverbs tell about love, gossip, and malicious words?

   17:9 _____

   _____

   _____

   10:12 _____

   _____

   16:28 _____

   _____

   26:20-22 _____

   _____

   _____

Discussion Questions: How do you think we can demonstrate love that covers over sin? What do these verses reveal about the nature of gossip? What is revealed when you gossip about another?

It is important to realize that love covers over sin. One action that is contrary to the covering over of sin is gossip, and it is a dangerous action. The gossip delights in "uncovering" the faults of others. The person who loves does not want others to know about the faults and shortcomings of the one she loves. Love can make a person blind to another's faults.

Read **Titus 3:1-5.**

12. What instructions regarding our speech are found in verse 2?

_____

_____

13. How is the unbeliever described (v. 3)?

_____

_____

_____

14. What attributes of God are given in verses 4, 5?

_____

_____

Read **Titus 3:5-11.**

15. What has God done for us (vv. 5-7)?

_____

_____

_____

_____

16. Why did God do these things for us?

_____

Discussion Question: How do these verses demonstrate the love of God that covers over sin?

17. What should the believer be careful to do and why (v. 8)?

_____

_____

_____

18. What should be avoided and why?

_____

_____

19. What does verse 11 tell about a person who causes divisions?

_____

Discussion Questions: How can gossip and foolish arguments contribute to divisions within a church or family? What can we do to prevent gossip?

If we are going to love as Jesus loved, we must refuse to allow ourselves to become part of gossip sessions. The tales that we hear become a part of the way we think of others. The more we gossip and complain about a person's faults, the worse they will seem to become. Our love should cover over sin rather than magnify it.

Read **1 Corinthians 13:4-7.**
20. What phrases relate to love that covers over or to gossip?

_____

21. What phrases speak of patience as an action of love?

_____

_____

Read **James 5:7-11.**
22. How long are we encouraged to be patient?

_____

23. What three examples of patience are given in this passage?

_____

Discussion Questions: How does this passage define patience? How is a farmer an example of patience? How are Job and the prophets examples?

24. What is encouraged in verse 8 and why?

_____

_____

25. What action contrary to patience are we to avoid and why?

_____

26. Why were the prophets regarded as happy or blessed?

_____

Read **Job 42:10-17.**
27. How did God reward Job's patience?

_____

_____

We often think that being patient means that we will never lose our tempers. Patience will often help us to control our anger, but in this scripture we see that patience is defined as endurance. Often it is hard to remain in a difficult marriage or other relationship. Many people are quick to leave a marriage that they find does not meet their needs. It is often easier to leave a church or dissolve a friendship than it is to work on correcting problems. God's kind of love does not give up. Love seeks a solution and keeps trying.

28. Read the following verses. List instructions and promises found in each.

Gal. 6:8-10 _____

_____

_____

_____

Heb. 4:14-16 _____

_____

_____

_____

_____

Prov. 16:7 _____

_____

_____

Prov. 21:21 _____

_____

Discussion Question: Which promise from these verses is most meaningful to you?

There are times when it is easy to become discouraged and the desire to give up can be very strong. If you are struggling with discouragement, find a promise from God that applies to your situation. Memorize that promise, write it down and place it where you will see it often and be reminded that this is God's promise to you. Claim His promise. Personalize it. Remember that His love for you is a love that never gives up. It is His will for you to love as Jesus has loved us. God wants to give you the strength to love with a love that doesn't give up.

Personal Questions: Will you ask God to give you a love that doesn't give up? Will you ask Him for power to love even during difficult circumstances?

Read **1 Thessalonians 3:12,13.**
29.   What is requested in this prayer?

_____

_____

_____

30.   What would be the result?

_____

_____

_____

Personal Application
1. Rewrite the words of these verses making them your prayer to God.
2. Make the promises your promises from God.

Memory Work
"He who covers over an offense promotes love, but whoever repeats the matter separates close friends" (Prov. 17:9).